A Short Book of Bad Judges

A SHORT BOOK OF
BAD JUDGES

GRAEME WILLIAMS

Queen's Counsel,
A Senior Bencher of The Inner Temple,
Formerly A Recorder of The Crown Court, ETC.

Wildy, Simmonds & Hill Publishing

© Graeme Williams, 2013

ISBN: 9780854901418

British Library Cataloguing
in Publication Data

A catalogue record for this book
is available from the British Library

First published in 2013 by Wildy, Simmonds & Hill Publishing
58 Carey Street London WC2A 2JF England www.wildy.com

Printed in Great Britain by
CPI Antony Rowe, Chippenham, Wiltshire.

MIX
Paper from
responsible sources
FSC
www.fsc.org
FSC® C013604

Contents.

Table of Cases

Acknowledgements

I WISH TO RECORD MY GRATITUDE TO THE FOLLOWING, all of whom have helped me in various ways in the writing of this book, and my apologies also to those whose names I have by oversight omitted:-

Margaret Clay, Librarian, and her staff at the Inner Temple Library;

Simon Blundell, the Librarian of the Reform Club, where my wife is a member, and I am frequently her guest;

Lindsay Merriman, daughter of the late Sir Robert Megarry, for her kind permission to use much material from her father's book, *A New Miscellany-at-Law*, chapter 2, for my Chapter 2;

Sir Martin Nourse, P.C., for helpful information about Lords Trevethin and Oaksey;

Clare Schneider, for her help and expertise with computing;

Vicky Wharton, for very expert help with lay-out and design, and numerous long-suffering and excellent suggestions, and the cover;

Dr Brian Hill, of Wildys, most patient of publishers;

Bernard Richmond, QC, for the use and benefit of his research into judicial misbehaviour;

The Honourable Society of the Inner Temple and Ian Jones, for their kind permission to use the photograph of the painting of the Court of King's Bench;

Emma Butterfield at the National Portrait Gallery, for much patient help with the illustrations, and generous permission to use them;

And most particularly, Anna Worrall, QC, my dear wife of over fifty years (much fewer than when I began this work), who has patiently accepted my work on the book as an alibi for more urgent and important domestic tasks, and allowed me to use, and abuse, her computer.

Prologue and Apology

THERE ARE PLENTY OF BOOKS ABOUT Good English Judges: indeed their goodness may well have been one of their authors' main reasons for writing them. But, so far as I, or Google know, there is as yet no book specifically about Bad Judges in this country, though there are quite a few in the United States. No doubt there are a number of reasons for this: the law of Libel, within its limits, protects the living, and the old maxim 'de mortuis nil nisi bonum' may protect the dead, at least for a decent interval 'post mortem'. In addition, the recent material for this book in England & Wales is laudably scarce: Scotland must speak for itself.

There are now here, south of the Border, and there have recently been, many fewer Bad Judges than in the past, even though there are now a lot more judges, at every level, than there were as lately as fifty years ago. In Chapter 2 we shall follow one judge overseas, but only within the Empire, at a time when the U.K. provided Judges world-wide. Sir Robert Megarry (in his marvellous Miscellanies-at-Law) and Lord (David) Pannick QC (in his excellent book, 'Judges' – not to be confused with the less entertaining Old Testament Book of the same name) have both adopted a discursive, and wider ranging, study of judges, old and new, 'home and away' good, bad and peculiar. I have attempted a much briefer, more domestic and biographical approach, specifically to Bad Judges.

The position here today is no doubt the result of our modern, and on the whole very sensible and worth-while, practice of appointing 'new' permanent judges only after they have attended judicial training, have sat as judge in a part-time, temporary judicial post before appointment, and have performed in that capacity well enough to justify long-term judicial office. But as we shall see, this usually safe system is not wholly free from error. The unhappy American experience may perhaps be attributable to the system, in many States, of electing, rather than appointing, judges. Incidentally, much the same may be said, for the time being at least, of the comparative methods of selecting the members of our two Houses of Parliament. But I must not lead myself into that perennial controversy.

Moreover, as readers of John Milton and Beatrix Potter will know, reading about bad characters tends to be much more fun than reading about good ones. I confess to thinking that Paradise Lost and the Tales of Mr Tod, and of Two Bad Mice are all more entertaining to read than Paradise Regained or the Flopsy Bunnies; and I have found that the same is true about writing about judges. So this is my Prologue and Explanation.

Introduction

No DOUBT I OUGHT, AT THIS EARLY STAGE, to attempt some sort of at least provisional definition of a bad Judge; and to ask the twin questions which need to be asked, and if possible answered, before we examine particular instances:-

What makes a bad Judge? Or what makes a Judge bad?

It is presumably the case that some Judges are born bad, and some achieve badness; but have any had badness thrust upon them? We shall see. What can be said at once is that being a bad lawyer is neither necessary nor sufficient. A Bad Judge may be a good or bad lawyer. He (laudably, seldom she) usually forgets that the most important person in Court is, certainly not him or her, or even, as some contend, the Court Usher, but is the losing litigant.

Luckily for me, many of these questions were elegantly answered in the 17th century by that versatile man, Lord (Francis) Bacon (1561-1626). He found time to write (when not also writing plays under the nom-de-plume of 'William Shakespeare') a very successful and influential book, called:-

'The Essayes or Counsels, Civill and Morall; Of Judicature', from whose 3rd edition of 1625 I will quote, but only 'at second hand' (that is, from another, and also very distinguished, source; sc. Lord Justice Denning, see page 43 below).

'Patience and gravity of hearing is an essential part of justice: and an over-speaking judge is no well-tuned cymbal.'[1]

1 A reference, of course, to Psalm 150; Verse 5; but how do you tune a cymbal?

The quotation from Bacon continues as follows as a footnote in [1957] 2 WLR 766 (vide infra), but oddly not in the fuller report at [1957] 2 QB 155. Non-lawyers may be excused from reading it, even though it is well worth the trouble:-

> 'It is no grace to a judge first to find that which he might have heard in due time from the bar, or to show quickness of conceit in cutting off evidence or counsel too short; or to prevent information by questions, though pertinent. The parts of a judge in hearing are four: to direct the evidence, to moderate length, repetition, or impertinency of speech; to recapitulate, select and collate the material points or that which hath been said; and to give the rule or sentence. Whatsoever is above these is too much; and proceedeth either of glory and willingness to speak, or of impatience to hear or of shortness of memory, or of want of a staid and equal attention...but...let not the judge meet the cause half way, nor give occasion for the party to say his counsel or his proofs were not heard.'

I very respectfully agree that, not far short of 500 years later, impatience is still the most common fault in the judicial character, though its consequence is usually to lengthen, not to shorten, the hearing. Even with experienced advocates in front of him, it can be perilously easy for a less than patient judge to suppose that he knows better than both, or all, of the lawyers before him, what the case is about, and what the solution is. This trap has very recently become much more dangerous, as an easily foreseeable result of the now severely reduced availability of Legal Aid to individual litigants. This is having the obvious consequent increase in unrepresented litigants appearing in Court 'in person' (even in the highest Courts) towards whom almost limitless patient judicial indulgence must be shown, whilst not giving to the other party, whether or not represented by a competent lawyer, an impression of excessive judicial sympathy for the lay litigant.

This is not always an easy balance to strike, as I discovered for myself when sitting to hear civil and family cases in the Crown and County Courts.

Supposed omniscience, and all-too-real pomposity, are two other defects that can tarnish the judicial performance. The first of these can be the result of over-long exposure to the same kind of, or even to the very same, litigants, or advocates. The second is more likely to affect a recently appointed Judge, who may find the sometimes excessive sycophancy of the lawyers, and even his own new robes, too much to his liking.

It is fair to say that, much as one swallow does not make a summer, nor one redwing (an avian winter visitor) a winter, one badly conducted case does not make a judge bad. Human nature, or even a row with one's spouse the night before, may 'excuse' an isolated fall from judicial grace, and fall short of earning a judge the badge of Badness: we all have our 'off days'. But several or repeated, or even habitual, instances of bad judicial behaviour must be more serious. Even so, one really bad case can exemplify a bad judicial temperament.

Another related judicial failing, which has given rise to many successful appeals and quashed criminal convictions, is excessive intervention, especially in the questioning of witnesses. The classic statement of principle, often referred to in other cases, was made in the 'strong' case of *Yuill* v. *Yuill* [1945] P. 15 at p.20 by that famously Good Judge, Lord Greene M.R.:-

'A judge who observes the demeanour of the witnesses while they are being examined by counsel has from his detached position a much more favourable opportunity of forming a just appreciation than a judge who himself conducts the examination. If he takes the latter course he, so to speak, descends into the arena and is liable to have his vision clouded by the dust of the conflict. Unconsciously he deprives himself of the advantage of calm and dispassionate observation.'

The metaphor of 'descent into the arena' is very apt and has very often been adopted by other judges. In that case the Court of Appeal took the very unusual decision to reverse the trial judge's conclusion on the reliability of the evidence of witnesses whom the judge (Wallington J.) had heard and seen, but whom, the Court of Appeal held, the judge had taken an excessive part in questioning.

There are, I think, at least three easily distinguished kinds of Badness in Judges; there may be others. First, happily very rare, is the conviction of a Judge of a serious criminal offence. In the '70s, Judge Bruce Campbell, a former Family Law practitioner and by then a Circuit Judge, pleaded Guilty to attempting illicitly to import a substantial quantity of whisky and cigarettes. He was peremptorily dismissed, having unsuccessfully tried to resign, by Lord Chancellor Hailsham.

A far more senior and respected Judge, Lord Justice (Charles) Russell, was luckier. He had pleaded Guilty to driving home from his train station in rural Surrey, being appreciably over the, then recently introduced, permissible alcohol limit. He had ignored the station staff's advice not to drive. A few days after the local Court hearing, at which he was of course disqualified from driving, he is reputed to have asked the President of the three-man Court of Appeal in which he was to sit, Lord Justice (Arthian) Davies (always known as 'Beetle' because of his use of numerous pairs of spectacles), 'What should I do, Beetle?' To which question Beetle is said to have given the terse answer 'Sit tight, Charles'. Sir Charles sat tight, and survived; indeed, he was a few years later even granted a life peerage and promoted to sit in the House of Lords.[2]

I doubt if that would have happened under Hailsham's successor, the much-admired, Lord Mackay of Clashfern: indeed I think he made an overt policy statement that a judge, of whatever rank from lay magistrate upwards, who failed the Breathalyser test, or committed anything other than a very minor traffic offence, was expected to resign or be dismissed. In my respectful view, an entirely proper policy.

The second, and by far the most common, form of badness, is the misconduct of cases in Court. This may arise from dislike of one or more of the advocates before him, or from dislike of the way the case is being conducted, or from our old friend (and Judge's enemy) Impatience, or from sheer boredom with the, often tedious and repetitive, job of Judging. We shall see quite a few of these hereafter.

The third, last, and rarest, form of badness arises from the misconduct in one of the administrative and judicial functions, many involving subordinate judicial appointments, which some particularly senior judges are called upon to exercise. Lord Chancellor Westbury is our only occupant of this, rather exclusive bell-jar: see Chapter 1 below.

No doubt there are, or will be, other categories. But I think we have enough by now to be going on with. Some readers may be disappointed not to find their own 'favourite' bad Judge omitted from these pages: I have deliberately called the book 'Short'. I make no claim to have included all possible candidates; a mere list of names, or of more discreet initials, would not be very interesting. So I have confined myself to ten judges, whose badness has been authenticated, and has had interesting or even amusing consequences.

The reactions of those of my barrister, or ex-barrister,

2 Robert Stevens: The Independence of the Judiciary; Oxford; 1993, page 166.

friends to whom I have mentioned my plan to write this book, have fallen into two groups. A few have expressed surprise that I could find enough bad judges to make a worthwhile, even explicitly 'Short', book; others, the majority, have said 'a Short Book of Bad Judges' is bound to be inadequate, there being so many to include. To both schools of thought I reply that, granted the constraints already referred to, I have included only those against whom there exists clear evidence, in the Law Reports or elsewhere, of one form of badness or another. Mere grumbles, however numerous and strongly held or expressed, I have not regarded as sufficient. I repeat: I do not claim to have included ALL the possible rogues in the gallery. I was much encouraged by the reaction of a very senior retired (Good) Judge, when I mentioned my proposal to him: 'That' he said 'is a book we need'. I can only hope I have gone some way to fill the need.

A quite recent problem, reported in The Times of 28th June 2012, raised the interesting questions of what should be the attitude of, and what steps (if any) should be taken by, an appellate Court which has to consider a ground of appeal making serious allegations against the conduct of the trial judge, such that the appellant did not have a fair trial. In the case there discussed, allegations of misconduct of a trial and of prejudicial remarks made, and questions asked, by the trial judge, a barrister of very high professional reputation, decorated in recognition of his services, (and elected to the Inner Temple Bench on the same day as I was), were made, and were accepted by the appellate Court; so the conviction was quashed. However it soon appeared that the appeal Court's version, and hence their opinion, of the trial judge's conduct was vigorously challenged, as being 'unrecognisable', by other counsel in the trial, who had not been involved in the appeal, and indeed by the Judge. The serious questions arose: what rights, if any, has a trial judge to be heard in relation to crucial allegations (which he may well, and in that case did, dispute) against a judge's professional conduct made by a dissatisfied litigant, including a defendant in a criminal case? And what steps can or should an appellate Court take to resolve any such dispute? The most unsatisfactory answer seems to be 'none'. Possibly the solution may lie with counsel for the prosecution, but alas even he cannot always be relied on to put the record straight, and in some cases may have decided not to support the conviction.

CHAPTER ONE

An Unpopular 19TH Century
Lord Chancellor

RICHARD BETHELL, THE FUTURE Lord Chancellor Westbury, was a remarkable man, who had a remarkable career. It is right that I should at the very outset acknowledge my debt, in most of what follows in this Chapter, to two fine accounts of his life: J.B.Atlay's in Chapters X to XIII in Volume II of his masterly two-volume work, 'The Victorian Chancellors', published in London and Boston (Mass.) in 1908, and R.C.J. Cocks' in Volume 5, of the Oxford Dictionary of National Biography; hereafter ODNB, dated 2004 (sub nomine Bethell).

The outline of his early career is worth tracing, in view of what followed. He was born in June 1800; his father was a far from wealthy doctor in Bradford-upon-Avon. He was educated in the classics at a private school in Bristol, and by his father at home. He was extremely precocious. His father took him at the age of 14 to Wadham College, Oxford, where he was (exceptionally) admitted; in his first year he won both a scholarship and an exhibition. In his fourth year, at the age of 17, he began to teach private pupils; he later claimed to be financially independent of his father thereafter. He obtained a first-class degree in classics and a second class (there were then only two classes) in mathematics. He stayed at Oxford for 4 more years, winning the Vinerian Law Scholarship, being elected a Fellow of Wadham College, and joining the Middle Temple as a law student.

Then he came to London to study Law, and was called to the Bar in 1823 by the Middle Temple. He was a pupil of an, I think, now extinct subspecies at the Bar, an equity draftsman. He joined a distinguished set of chambers at 9 New Square, Lincoln's Inn, at which address the author, Atlay himself, was to begin practice many years later.

It was at this stage that his behaviour began to attract adverse comment from his colleagues. Atlay cautiously attributes (at page 223) his nickname 'Miss Fanny' to his 'mincing manner and refinement of intonation (and) the stately and elaborate form of speech in which his most trivial sentences were clothed (which) produced the impression of affectation;...' He made what can now be seen as the mistakes of using these characteristics in being both sarcastic at the expense of any adversary, including judges, and, worse still, almost always right. I think most of us will have come across very able people like him, who can be easy to admire, but hard to befriend. But these problems did not prevent him from marrying, in 1826, a Miss Abraham, the daughter of a prominent architect. This step required him to forfeit his College Fellowship; (in this respect at least Oxford has moved forward). She bore him several sons, two of whom were in different ways to be instrumental in his eventual downfall from office, as we shall see.

His very first client was my old college, Brasenose. They won the case, which all the other lawyers of greater standing, whom they had consulted advised them they would lose, and an appeal[3] by their opponents, in which Bethell was led by Sugden Q.C. (the future Lord Chancellor

3 *A-G v Brasenose College*(1834) 2 C. & F.295. Atlay asserts (p.224) that the College Principal caused him to be instructed because he recalled Bethell's felicitous translation of a strophe of Pindar in the viva voce examination for his degree some years earlier: a striking example of the mysterious reasons for early success at the Bar. What better reason could there be?

St. Leonards), was dismissed.

Thereafter he quickly built up a busy Equity practice in the 1820s and '30s; he took silk in 1840. He rapidly achieved a dominant and lucrative position at the Chancery Bar, the result of his own very hard and expert work, and of the appointment to the Bench, or the retirement, or death, of his colleagues and competitors. He had been very pleased to be appointed standing counsel to Oxford University in 1846.

The path of ambition led him into politics, but without any great political commitment; he was unsuccessful in his first attempt, but in 1851 he won a by-election at Aylesbury. His Parliamentary activities mainly involved reform of legal, especially Chancery, procedure in which he was, of course, an expert. He also promoted the neglected functions of the Inns of Court in teaching law to their students, and was one of the first presidents of the Council of Legal Education; only at this time were formal Bar Examinations made compulsory. He retained the seat at a General Election in 1852, and accepted the post of Solicitor-General, and a Knighthood. I do not think the details of his meteoric Parliamentary career thereafter need detain us here, save to say that he rose to be Attorney-General in 1856. In that capacity he was charged with promoting the, then very controversial, Divorce Bill (which became the Divorce and Matrimonial Causes Act, 1857)[4] against strong, but unavailing, opposition from Gladstone, inter alios.

When Lord Chancellor Chelmsford (né Thesiger) first left office in 1859, Bethell hoped to succeed him; but Palmerston appointed 'Jock' Campbell, the 79 year-old Lord Chief Justice; he promised Bethell the job at the next vacancy. This did not please everybody: Lord Grandville described Bethell as 'clever but coxcombical'.

---

4 Parts of this important Act remained in force until 1965.

He did not have long to wait: Campbell died in office after less than two years, and Palmerston kept his promise. Bethell became Lord Chancellor in June 1861, and took the title Baron Westbury, a town in Wiltshire, known to me otherwise only as being served in the last century by a slip-carriage on the main Great Western railway line. (see illustations 1 and 2)

Westbury's period as Lord Chancellor was notable, apart from the manner of its ending, in particular for his part in an extraordinary, and typically high Victorian, piece of litigation. In 1860 two clergymen published a book, innocuously entitled 'Essays and Reviews', which contained two articles, which threw doubt (first) on the direct authorship, or at least inspiration, by Almighty God of every word of the Bible, and (second) on the doctrine of the everlasting, and irremediable, damnation of sinners.

These two contentions attracted the unfavourable attention of the then Bishop of Salisbury, Samuel Wilberforce, an inveterate conservative controversialist (always known as 'Soapy Sam'; see illustration 3). He is better known to history as a vigorous opponent of Charles Darwin and the Theory of Evolution by Natural Selection; but he threw his considerable energies also into his disapprobation of the authors of the articles in 'Essays and Reviews', Dr Rowland Williams (no relation, so far as I know!) and the Rev. H. B. Wilson. He caused the two clergymen to be suspended from their offices for twelve months by the respected authority, Dr Lushington, the Dean of Arches. They appealed to the Privy Council, in which Westbury presided over the two Archbishops, the Bishop of London, and three distinguished lawyers.

The appeal was triumphantly allowed, the two 'heretics' were reinstated and Soapy Sam was discomfited. It is true,

Lord Westbury from a photograph of 1800 looking stately and self satisfied?

"An eminent Christian man."

Lord Westbury By 'Ape'. Looking mischievous - 1869

'Soapy' Sam Wilberforce By 'Ape'. Looking saponiferous.

as the books assert, that the two arch-bishops dissented, but close examination of the report shows that their dissents were only partial, and each on different points.[5] So the decision was virtually unanimous.

Westbury delivered the Board's very learned judgment, dealing with ecclesiastical law of much antiquity. This prompted an extraordinary and ironical, but anonymous, 'jeu d'esprit' in the form of a premature mock funerary inscription (too long to quote here in full) but including the following:-

'RICHARD, BARON WESTBURY.

LORD HIGH CHANCELLOR OF ENGLAND.

HE WAS AN EMINENT CHRISTIAN,

AN ENERGETIC AND MERCIFUL STATESMAN,

AND A STILL MORE EMINENT AND MERCIFUL JUDGE.

DURING HIS THREE YEARS' TENURE OF OFFICE

HE ABOLISHED..........THE ETERNITY OF PUNISHMENT.

TOWARDS THE CLOSE OF HIS EARTHLY CAREER

IN THE JUDICIAL COMMITTEE OF THE PRIVY COUNCIL

HE DISMISSED HELL WITH COSTS,

AND TOOK AWAY FROM ORTHODOX MEMBERS

OF THE CHURCH OF ENGLAND

THEIR LAST HOPE OF EVERLASTING DAMNATION.'

The Judicial Committee's judgment, and Lord Westbury's vigorous defence of it, brought down upon his head a storm of public abuse, stirred up by 'Soapy Sam' Wilberforce, who persuaded the Convocation of Canterbury to make

---

5   see the report of *Williams v. Bishop of Salisbury* (1864) 2 Moo. P.C. (N.S.) 375, A pleasantly absurd Law Report reference, which I have waited a professional life-time to use; 'Moo' is a ludicrous abbreviation of the reporter's name; he was Edmund F. Moore.

a 'synodical judgment' condemning the book as 'heretical'. This in turn elicited a scornful riposte from Westbury, who in Parliament described the Convocation's Judgment as 'a well-lubricated set of words, a sentence so oily and saponaceous that no one could grasp it. Like an eel, it slips through your fingers': an extreme example of Westbury's wounding sarcasm, obviously aimed at Wilberforce. Atlay (at page 267) describes this episode as 'a serious blunder' by Westbury, possibly presaging his imminent disgrace. The whole episode seems to me to show how extraordinarily different from today's public controversies were those of 150 years ago: the past is, indeed, 'a foreign country'.

Westbury's fall from grace came about in this way. In the first place, a certain Mr Edmunds held two pensionable positions, one in the House of Lords and the other in the Patent Office, both under the Lord Chancellor's control. In the course of a review instigated by Westbury in 1865, it came to light that Edmunds had mismanaged, to his own advantage, a substantial sum of public funds in the Patent Office job; for this it was proposed that he be charged with the appropriate offences. He applied to Westbury to be allowed to resign and keep his valuable pension, if he repaid the proceeds of his defaults. Westbury rashly agreed to this. But Edmunds, as is the way with fraudsters, repaid only some, but less than half, of his 'winnings'.

Further Westbury agreed to allow him, if the House of Lords consented, to resign with the pension from the other, Parliamentary, position. Here he made two more mistakes: he failed to inform the relevant committee of the House of Lords of Edmunds' previous dishonesty at the Patent Office, and, worse, he appointed his son Slingsby to the now vacant House of Lords' job. There was predictable uproar in the

Press. Westbury offered his resignation, but, for political reasons, the Prime Minister, Palmerston refused to accept it.

In the second place, Westbury's laudable review of the law and practice of Insolvency, as administered in the provincial District Registries, threw up a number of abuses, one the worst of which involved a man named Wilde at the Leeds District Registry. As in Edmunds' case, Wilde asked to be allowed to resign with a pension, if he could provide medical evidence of ill health. Once again Westbury agreed, at the instigation of a Mr Cooper, the Chief Bankruptcy Registrar; relying on weak medical evidence, he allowed Wilde to escape the proper consequences of his abuse of office, and to resign and retain his pension. Westbury thereupon appointed a barrister called Welch to fill the vacancy. This seemed satisfactory, until it emerged that Welch had lent substantial sums of money to Westbury's spendthrift eldest son, also named Richard, and himself bankrupt! It seems that there had been an elaborate plot, involving Wilde, Cooper, Welch and Richard, jnr; and that Westbury had allowed himself to be deceived. He again offered to resign and Palmerston again refused.

The 'coup de grace' was administered in July 1865, when an Opposition Front Bench M.P. moved a formal vote of censure against the Lord Chancellor for inter alia 'want of caution' in his office. It was at this late stage that the chickens of his past disagreeable behaviour came home to roost; Palmerston tried to get the debate on the censure motion adjourned, but Westbury's unpopularity was such that the House of Commons refused to grant any adjournment, and Palmerston was obliged to agree to the motion of censure against Westbury, which obviously made his position as Lord Chancellor untenable.

Atlay at page 273 gives a dramatic account of the news being carried aftermidnight by a messenger on horseback to

Westbury's 'country' residence in Lancaster Gate, in the form of a message from the Prime Minister, at last accepting Westbury's resignation from the office of Lord Chancellor. On 6th July he made a moving final speech from the Woolsack to a crowded House of Lords. By a bitter irony, on the following day, when he travelled to Windsor to deliver up the Great Seal to Queen Victoria, he encountered his old adversary, Bishop Wilberforce. No words were exchanged, but Soapy Sam noted that he looked 'quite down'. They were later at least partly reconciled.

Strangely, to my way of thinking, his resignation, and the reasons for it, did not wholly terminate Westbury's legal and judicial career. After a decent interval spent in Tuscany, he resumed sitting, and even on occasion presiding, to hear appeals in the House of Lords and the Judicial Committee. No doubt he would have avoided having to hear Indian Appeals, which he used to disparage with the, today unacceptable, description of 'curry and chutnee'. He continued his efforts in Parliament to simplify the law by legislative codification [he had always held 'judge-made law' in low esteem], an ambition which some still pursue even today, but still without much success. He was a member, and later the Chairman, of a Royal Commission to consider making 'a digest of law'; like so many of its kind, this well-intentioned enterprise came to nothing.

His first wife had died in 1863; he remarried in 1873 to a Miss Tennant, he being as old as the century. But his health was failing. Even so he was appointed by a private Act of Parliament to inquire into, and resolve, for a substantial fee, the huge legal and factual problems arising from the dubious insolvency of the European Assurance Society, a precursor of several modern financial scandals. As his health worsened, the hearing had to be moved to the dining room of his private house, where he sat with a grandson standing behind him holding a bag of ice to the back of his neck, to relieve the constant pain he was suffering.

He completed the case, but died soon after, early on 20th July 1873. He had managed to outlive Soapy Sam by only about 12 hours; the bishop had died in full health and vigour, on being thrown from his horse the day before.

Bethell was obviously a complex man. Intellectually brilliant and socially abrasive, but strongly ambitious, ruthless, and careless of the feelings of others. His profession downfall was caused, not by personal dishonesty, but by a surprising naivety and misjudgment of other people, and (as one of his contemporaries put it) his 'fatuous simplicity' in failing to suspect, or detect, dishonesty in others, which he would have readily spotted in his forensic or judicial capacity.

In this respect, if not as a lawyer, he was in my view manifestly a Bad Judge.

Two Extraordinary 19TH Century Judges: Willis and Ramshay

IN BEGINNING THIS CHAPTER I MUST, AND DO, at once acknowledge my debt to the late Sir Robert Megarry and his daughter Lindsay, now Mrs Merriman, (once upon a time a pupil in my former chambers). She has very kindly allowed me to make extensive use of her father's work), as I have for the material contained in Chapter 2 of 'A New Miscellany-at-Law' edited by Bryan A. Garner and published in 2005. That chapter, and indeed the rest of the book, bear the inimitable signs of Sir Robert's remarkable knowledge of, and tireless research into, the by-ways of the common law and its practitioners. It is at least as much of a joy to read, and marvel at, as were its two precursors: Miscellany-at-Law and A Second Miscellany-at-Law, of 1955 and 1973 respectively.

JOHN WILLIS

The Judges in question, John Willis and William Ramshay, are both notable in at least two respects, first for being very bad judges, and secondly for being themselves involved in litigation concerning their appointments. The latter is, so far as I know, a unique feature of their careers.

Willis comes first in time. He had a conventional English education at Rugby, Charterhouse (then in Smithfield in London, before it moved to Godalming) and Trinity Hall, Cambridge, was called to the Bar by Gray's Inn in 1816 at the age of 23, and practised at the Chancery Bar for only about ten years. Then at the early age of 34 he was appointed as a King's Bench Judge in 'Upper Canada', the future Ontario, where his tenure was brief. He expected to be transferred to a newly-established Chancery Court, but at once became involved in disputes with the Attorney-General of the Province, amongst others, about the Attorney's duties. He further made himself unpopular by applying, after less than a year in Canada, to become Chief Justice, when the then occupant of that post was about to retire, and by refusing to sit with a colleague as a Divisional Court in the Chief Justice's absence. These and other incidents, all within months of his arrival, led the Governor 'to amove[6]' him from office under the Colonial Leave of Absence Act, 1782.

He returned to England to challenge the Governor's decision in the Privy Council. He was, perhaps surprisingly, supported by the House of Assembly of Upper Canada. The Privy Council held that he was wrong to refuse to sit in the Divisional Court, but that the Governor had also been wrong to amove him without hearing from him in reply to the complaints against him: an elementary mistake.

But, although at least partly vindicated, he did not return to Canada. His next appointment was as Vice-President of the Court of Civil and Criminal Justice in, of all places, British Guiana: not, I would imagine, a very eagerly sought-after position. He was there for an even shorter time than he was in Canada, returning to England with chronic liver trouble (which cannot have improved his disposition) after a few months. His next, and last, job was even

---

6 Not a misprint, but a word, omitted from the Concise OED, but included in Section 2 of the Act and as 'obsolete' at p.412 of Vol. 1 of the current OED. It means, as one might expect, the same as 'to remove', hence its obsolescence, but it might be useful for Scrabble.

further from home: in 1837 he was appointed, despite his unpromising record, a Judge of the Supreme Court of New South Wales (an appellation which at that time applied to a much larger part of Australia than it does today). He is reported as having brought 43 tons of luggage with him, when he arrived in Melbourne in March 1841: travel by sea then allowed, but air travel would today have penalised, such amazing extravagance.

Problems soon arose between him, and his fellow judges, the local lawyers and the press such that, within a little over two years from his arrival, the same Act of 1782 was invoked by the Governor, Sir George Gipps, to amove him a second time and to revoke his appointment as Resident Judge of Port Phillip. He was further 'inhibited' from the exercise of all power and authority as a judge. The immediate cause of these steps is thought to have been his deplorable reaction to a judgment of the Full Court, reversing on appeal a decision of his. He had ordered a solicitor to be struck off the rolls; but, having been reversed, he chose to read aloud the Full Court's judgment in his Court, interspersed with insults towards the solicitor and the judges of the Full Court. He also refused to reinstate the solicitor.

Needless to say, he exercised his right of appeal to the Privy Council, with, very remarkably, much the same result as there had been following his Canadian misadventure; the orders were reversed. The Privy Council's decision is reported at *Willis v. Gipps* (1846) 5 Moo[7]. P.C. 379; he had given 'sufficient grounds for the amotion', but again had not been given any proper opportunity to be heard (the same elementary mistake, again), and so the decision was reversed. The report repays close examination. In the first place, the

7   Hallo again, Mr Moore!

Committee of the Privy Council hearing the appeal in June and July 1846 included, not only a number of well-known legal luminaries, such as Lord Brougham and Baron Parke, but also (to my astonishment) the Right Honourable W.E.Gladstone, who,so far as I know, had no formal legal expertise whatever. He of course had never held 'High Judicial Office', but that was not then required for membership of a panel of privy counsellors hearing a legal appeal.

Moreover, the leading counsel for Sir George Gipps was none other than Mr R. Bethell QC, (see Chapter 1 above): the world of Bad Judges seems to be a small one, even though Bethell was then on the side of the angels.

But the Authorities' patience had run out, and, having received substantial arrears of salary on the strength of the Privy Council's decision, Willis had his appointments revoked by the Secretary of State, he being then in his mid-50s. From that decision there was no appeal; but he survived another 30 pensionable years, dying in 1877.

Sir Robert Megarry cites a number of opinions of Willis' biographers, who express the views that he was 'quite unfitted for judicial office, (being) vain and conceited, quick-tempered and quarrelsome, vindictive in action and violent in language....' and ' irascible and tempestuous'; but also that he had 'a brilliant, scholarly mind (and) sound legal knowledge'. These latter views derive from an Address presented to him after his second amotion. So I think one may say of them, that their author was 'not upon oath', as Dr Johnson said of the authors of lapidary inscriptions, including himself, when he was taken to task for his over-complimentary memorial words for Oliver Goldsmith.

On any view Willis was a really Bad Judge.

WILLIAM RAMSHAY

William Ramshay was even worse. He was appointed Judge of the Lancashire County Court by the Earl of Carlisle, as Chancellor of the Duchy of that County in April 1850. Ramshay's father and grandfather had both worked as land agents for the Earl.

Only fourteen months later the Earl held an Inquiry in London into the bad behaviour of the Judge, under Section 18 of the County Courts Act, 1846. The Liverpool Guardian Society complained that he used offensive language in Court and called parties and witnesses by opprobrious names, such as 'fools' and 'blockheads'. After 11 weeks, during which the Judge was forbidden to sit, the Chancellor decided not to remove him.

He celebrated this outcome by ordering some 150 cases to be listed for hearing at 9 a.m. five days later, but did not himself attend at Court untilnearly 1 p.m. (Not the way to gain the approval of the local lawyers, or their clients). He then made a number of insulting references to those who had, in his probably paranoid view, tried to have him removed. He also organised a banquet to be held in his Court 'in honour of the great principle of judicial independence, so long and recklessly assailed in this town'. The local full-time Liverpool Magistrate and the judge of the Cheshire County Court unwisely accepted invitations to this function, which was described by The Times as a 'most unseemly festival'; he perceived the local press as his main adversary.

The Liverpool Journal retaliated by causing a number of presumably hostile placards to be exhibited near the court, whereupon Ramshay ordered that the court bailiffs should bring the editor, a Mr Whitty, before him. The editor refused, unless he was validly summoned. Eventually, after a scuffle with the bailiffs and the issue of a summons, he attended with counsel, Sir George Stephen.

A very chaotic hearing ended with the judge imposing on Mr Whitty fines of '£5 each on 3 cases of assault' (apparently on the bailiffs) with seven days imprisonment each 'for two cases of assault', apparently, as Sir Robert says, in default of payment. Not surprisingly in the confrontational atmosphere Ramshay created, Mr Whitty did not pay, went to prison, but was 'released by subscriptions of his friends'.

Again not surprisingly, the Earl was soon asked by very numerous petitioners to remove the judge and appoint another 'of learning, temper, and moderation in his stead'. A long hearing took place at Preston over about 10 days in November 1851, involving a total of six counsel, and ending with the judge's removal, and appointment of a Mr Joseph Pollock (a surname held by a number of distinguished lawyers) in his place. But Ramshay was not finished yet; he declined to accept the Earl's decision. He purported to adjourn the next sitting of his former Court, but Mr, now Judge, Pollock ignored this impertinence, and sat in Court when he had proposed to. Ramshay tried to do the same a second time, but again failed.

His last resort was to begin 'quo warranto' proceedings in the Queen's Bench of the High Court to challenge the validity of Pollock's appointment. This too was unsuccessful: on 10th February 1851 Lord Chief Justice Campbell gave judgment upholding the Earl's decision[8]. At this point Ramshay disappears from history, leaving a striking record of Judicial Badness behind him.

---

8   Reported as *Ex parte Ramshay* (1852) 18 Q.B.173. We have, of course, already met Lord Campbell, as Lord Westbury's precursor as Lord Chancellor: see p10 supra.

CHAPTER THREE

A Very Bad 19th/20th Century
High Court Judge

In my previous, and first, venture into the writing of books, 'Death of a Circuit' in 2006, which was an account of the Last Days of the Oxford Circuit, I included a number of attacks upon Mr Justice Darling, who had been a member of that, now abolished, Circuit. Sir Michael Morland later told me that he thought I had been 'a bit hard on Darling'. So, in deference to Sir Michael, I have reviewed the material. I have to say that my unrepentant conclusion is that no book of Bad Judges would be worthy of its name if it did not include Charles Darling in a fairly prominent place.

He was born in 1849, into a moderately well-to-do middle-class family who inhabited first Abbey House, Colchester, and later Langham Hall, both in Essex. After an education at home but which did not include University, with the benefit of an inheritance from an uncle, he was articled to a firm of solicitors in Birmingham. He soon decided to come to the Bar, and he was called by the Inner Temple in 1874. He never had any significant practice. But he earned the gratitude of the Conservative Party at a General Election in 1888 by winning the unpromising seat at Deptford in the South London docks area, and holding it until 1897. He had taken silk in 1885. His proposed appointment to the High Court Bench by Lord Chancellor Halsbury in 1897 occasioned a remarkable burst of indignation in the professional, and the national, Press, including two hostile leading articles in The

Times and the following in the Solicitors' Journal for 1897:-

'Lord Halsbury has never shown his contempt for the opinion of the profession – and, we will add, of the Bench – so markedly as in his appointment of a successor to Lord Justice Henn Collins. The way to the High Court Bench is once more shown to be through contested elections and general service as a political hack. When these claims are present, learning, experience in practice, and the moral qualities which go to make an efficient and trusted judge are altogether unnecessary. We do not remember a more unanimous or sweeping condemnation than that with which the new appointment has been met by professional opinion.'

A similar blast was published in the Law Times for the same year. These prognostications were shown to be well justified after his appointment.

Professor Heuston, in his admirable chapters on Lord Halsbury (op. cit. p55) wrote of Darling:

'Although he possessed a ready and pleasant wit, he was incapable of resisting any opportunity of exercising it in public, and his court was filled with guffawing idlers …'

In other words, he lacked the 'gravity' which Lord Bacon regarded as essential in a judge. This lamentable trait gave rise to one of the cleverest ripostes imaginable, when, in a typically fatuous display of feigned 'judicial ignorance' he asked counsel, at the mention of the name of the most popular comedian of the day, 'Who is George Robey?' Quick as lightning came the brilliant reply (reputedly from Mr F. E. Smith QC, the future Lord Chancellor Birkenhead) 'My Lord, I believe he is the Darling of the Music Halls!'

Further reports of his bad behaviour in Court are to be found in C. P. Harvey's entertaining book, The Advocate's Devil, (1958 p33) and in Judge Bosanquet's book, The Oxford

Circuit, (1951 p107) who deplored Darling's conduct in the murder-by-poisoning case of Armstrong tried at Hereford Assizes. This latter comment contradicts the curious remark in the entry on Darling in both recent editions of the ODNB that 'in a murder trial he was very good', but it must be pointed out that, very ironically, the ODNB entry was written by Neville Laski, the notoriously Bad first Judge of the Crown Court at Liverpool, who has only escaped inclusion in this book for want of detailed material of his judicial badness. Laski describes Darling as 'small, gaunt and short-sighted. He, nonetheless, affected to a patrician hauteur in Court'. This latter 'affectation' is well caught in the haughty portrait by C.W. Furse in the National Portrait Gallery, painted in 1890 when Darling was still at the Bar: his smallness and gauntness seem to have escaped the painter's attention (see illustration on page opposite) a striking piece of self-regarding extravagance.

Laski's account is notable, not only for the moderation of what he includes, but also for one deplorable omission, which is Darling's most remarkable and lasting contribution to the Law: namely his quarrel with The Birmingham Daily Argus. I recounted this incident, quite briefly, in my previous publication 'Death of a Circuit' at page 59. The story is such a good one that I cannot resist repeating it here, this time in full, relying yet again on Sir Robert Megarry, whose account of it appeared in glorious detail in his (first) Miscellany-at-Law of 1955 at page 23. Darling had purported to warn the local newspapers against publishing some sexually explicit material relating to a trial of a man called Wells over which he was presiding in Birmingham. The Argus printed the following masterpiece of invective in March 1900:-

Mr Charles Darling, QC, MP, 1860, When Still At The Bar By C.W. Furze. Looking snooty.

'If anyone can imagine Little Tich upholding his dignity upon
a point of honour in a public house, he has a very fair concep-
tion of what Mr Justice Darling looked like in warning the
Press against the printing of indecent material. His diminutive
Lordship positively glowed with judicial self-consciousness. No
newspaper can exist except on its merits – a condition from which
the Bench, happily for Mr Justice Darling, is exempt. There is
not a journalist in Birmingham who has anything to learn from
the impudent little man in horsehair, a microcosm of conceit and
empty-headedness. One is almost sorry that the Lord Chancellor
had not another relative to provide for on the day he selected a
new judge from among the Larrikins of the law... One of Mr
Justice Darling's biographers states that "an eccentric relative 'left
him much money." That misguided testator [in fact, his uncle]
spoiled a successful bus conductor.'

For this the editor, a Mr Gray, was prosecuted for
Contempt of Court. It was, and is, very doubtful whether
abuse of a Judge (other than in Court, disrupting the proceedings) could as a matter of law amount to such a contempt,
or indeed whether it was proper or desirable for the Attorney-General to do what he did. In any event, the Court of
King's Bench, presided over by Lord Russell of Killowen,
was not called upon to decide any question of law, because
counsel for the editor did not seek to argue that his client's
conduct was not a contempt, and Mr Gray, having made what
can only be described as a grovelling apology, was fined £100
plus costs of £25.[9]

Worth every penny, old or new.

In the course of Darling's time as a Queen's, and later
a King's, Bench Judge he presided uneventfully over the
appeals of Dr Crippen and Roger Casement, and in the
important case of Chester v. Bateson [1920] 1 K.B., on the
validity of a war-time Regulation. In that case he saw fit to

9   Reported as R. v. Gray [1900] 2 Q.B.36

end his judgment with a, sans doute á propos, quotation in French from Montesquieu: pretentious, or what? He also passed a sensational sentence of imprisonment on Lady Ida Sitwell, Edith, Osbert, and Sacheverel Sitwell's aristocratic mother, when she was clearly the victim, and not the perpetrator, of a fraud.

He retired from the High Court Bench, with some ceremony, in November 1923. But strangely, after an unexplained 2-month hiatus, in January 1924 he was granted a peerage with the title Baron Darling of Langham. Never having sat in the Court of Appeal, but having been the senior judge of the King's Bench Division, after no less than 26 years' service there he thereafter sat in the House of Lords in its judicial capacity. It has been plausibly suggested to me that Darling was not, strictly speaking, 'a Law Lord', that is a Lord of Appeal in Ordinary; but was simply granted a peerage 'for good service', which, as we have seen, he had not given.

Apart from long service, there can hardly be any explanation (other than lingering political favouritism) for this seriously extraordinary step. As we have seen, his appointment to the High Court Bench occasioned an outcry of indignation, which had proved entirely justified by his conduct as a Judge of first instance.

There had, and have since, been a number of similar 'short cut' appointments; including one very recent, upon which judgment must at present be reserved. They have, I believe, all been made by reason of the merit of the individuals, as the names Radcliffe and Slynn attest. But if Darling's time as a puisne judge attested anything, it showed that he was conspicuously not of the intellectual, or indeed of the judicial, calibre, which might have justified his

Court of King's Bench in the late Middle Ages

'double' promotion. There were at the time, a number of Judges of the grand total of five *See Footnote 9 below* then in the Court of Appeal, where Darling had never been regarded as fit to sit, who were far better qualified for such promotion than Darling. Names such as Bankes, Scrutton and Atkin (who, after his promotion to the House of Lords in 1924, became one of the its most distinguished members in the 20th century) make the point without the need for further comment. What can Lord Chancellor Cave or the Prime Minister, Ramsay McDonald, have been thinking of? Darling's great supporter, Lord Halsbury, who had appointed him, had died over two years before.[10]

As Mr C. P. Harvey notes, his tiresome behaviour continued when sitting in the Lords; he describes an incident when Darling interrupted an elaborate legal argument in a tax appeal, with a fatuous joke involving the Compleat Angler, causing another Law Lord to drop a book in anger.

Darling was, however, a generous benefactor of his (and my) Inn, the Inner Temple. In particular he gave to the Inn a unique group of four very remarkable, small coloured pictures painted on vellum, of the four Courts of Justice, dating from about 1460. Now quite beyond price, they are brought out from safe storage and proudly displayed on the Inn's most festive occasions:

The Court is there depicted with 5 judges sitting in Westminster Hall 'in banc', wearing 'coifs' (not wigs). The accused is in the foreground with legs manacled and with an unpleasing-looking gaoler beside him. To left and right are two serjeants (senior barristers) also wearing coifs (not wigs); the jury is at the extreme left being sworn in by a court officer. Various clerks sit at the table below the Judges. The

10 There are now at the time of writing upwards of 40, depending on whom you count.

coats of arms include, I think, French fleurs de lys, quartered with English lions.

Darling retired from any Judicial work in 1930 and died in 1936.

He was notoriously a very Bad Judge.

CHAPTER FOUR

A Very Bad 20TH Century
Lord Chief Justice

GORDON HEWART MUST BE INCLUDED IN THIS BOOK, if only because he was roundly described by Prof. Heuston (op. cit. p.603) as 'perhaps the worst Lord Chief Justice since the seventeenth century'. That he was also a Bad Judge is a very widely held opinion, probably the only dissentient being his hagiographical biographer, R. Jackson in 'the Chief' of 1959.

He was born in Lancashire in 1870, educated at Manchester Grammar School and University College, Oxford, where he got a scholarship. He was called to the Bar by Inner Temple in 1902, joined the Northern Circuit, and took silk only 10 years later. He was Treasurer of his Inn in 1938. He had entered politics, being elected MP for Leicester East, in 1913. He became Solicitor-General in 1916 and Attorney-General in 1919. He was an active Freemason and a member of several Lodges. He had no judicial experience at all.

At that time there was a peculiar, and thoroughly undesirable, convention that, when the office of Lord Chief Justice became vacant, the Attorney-General at the time, whoever he happened to be, was 'entitled' to fill the vacancy. This obviously made the post of Chief Justice a matter of chance, much like musical chairs, and could give the job a wholly inappropriate political slant; moreover the A-G would be unlikely to have the judicial experience, nowadays regarded as essential for such an important job. But these considerations were obviously not regarded as important in the early

20th century, (though I think the convention made a another brief and ineffective reappearance, when Lord Parker retired and Sir Reginald Manningham-Buller [later Lord Dilhorne] was A-G, and hoped, in vain, to become Chief Justice). When the Lord Chief Justice Lord Reading (the former Rufus Isaacs QC) left the office to become British Ambassador to the U.S.A., Hewart expected, and thought he had the right, to succeed him.

However the Prime Minister of the day (Lloyd George) did not wish to lose Hewart's services as Attorney-General, and so an extraordinary, and in Lord Birkenhead's reported opinion illegal, device was employed to enable Hewart to fulfil his ambition, but not yet. Another Judge, A.T.Lawrence, a 77-year old puisne[11] of no great distinction, was approached with a view to his being appointed Lord Chief Justice, on condition that he provided a signed, but undated, letter of resignation. Thus it was possible for him to be 'sacked' whenever his superiors wanted. Remarkably, he agreed to this humiliating proposal, and took the title of Lord Trevethin[12]. It is said that he later read of his own resignation in The Times newspaper in March 1922, after only just over 12 months in office, when the government led by Lloyd George, by which Hewart had been appointed, lost a general election. On the 24th of that month Hewart became Lord Chief Justice, with no judicial experience whatsoever, an appointment inconceivable today.

11 Darling is said to have offered his services, when Isaacs resigned; and when Lawrence was appointed, Darling facetiously said he supposed he was, at 72, not old enough.

12 Trevethin's younger son also came to the Bar; was appointed to the High Court Bench, then to the Court of Appeal, and, as Lord Oaksey, to the House of Lords. In that capacity he served, with Lord (Norman) Birkett, as aBritish Judge at the Nuremburg Trial of the Nazi leaders in 1945, where their legal and diplomatic skills were very highly regarded. Lord Oaksey's son and heir was a noted expert on the Turf: he died recently.

The almost unanimous opinion of the Bar, the legal historians, and indeed his fellow judges and peers was that Hewart's was a disastrous appointment. In Mr C.P. Harvey's opinion [op. cit. p.34]: 'He lacked only the one quality which should distinguish a judge: that of being judicial. He remained the perpetual advocate'. He would form a view of a case at a very early stage, and would be apparently incapable of changing his mind thereafter.

Mr Robert Stephens, in the entry in Vol.26 of the ODNB, wrote: 'He was boorish and rude to counsel (and) to his fellow judge and had an infelicitous lack of judgment.'[13] He quarrelled with Lord Sankey, the Lord Chancellor in the House of Lords, and with Sankey's Permanent Secretary, Sir Claud Schuster, over some supposed slight relating to the alleged curtailment of his (Hewart's) authority. In addition to his other defects, he seems to have suffered from a tendency to paranoia, being preoccupied, even obsessed, with the notion that there was a conspiracy of civil servants in the Office of the Lord Chancellor, and elsewhere, to deprive him of his rightful powers and jurisdiction. This found expression in his book, published in 1929 entitled 'The New Despotism', in which he complained inter alia of the failure of the Civil Service to allow the appointment of additional King's Bench judges.

His personal attack, during a debate in the House of Lords, upon Claud Schuster was a clear and shocking breach of convention whereby a civil servant must not be personally criticised, because he is forbidden to reply in self-defence. Hewart was himself severely rebuked for this by Lord Hailsham, a former Lord Chancellor.

His total want of judicial experience, and of common courtesy, were amply demonstrated in the trial, over which

13 : see Stevens op. cit. p.32 seq . Hence two authoritative comentators have described him as lacking judicial qualities; a fundamental defect in a Chief Justice!

he presided in 1929, of two libel actions brought by a Mr Hobbs against The Nottingham Journal and Tinling & Co. Ltd, proprietors of the Liverpool Evening Express. [I hope what follows will not be too wearisome for my readers, be they lawyers or normal human beings; it amply demonstrates how impossible Hewart was as a trial judge.] These actions were two of a large number of claims for damages for libel made by Hobbs, a disreputable litigant, after his release from prison for a serious offence of blackmail against an Indian potentate.

Hobbs claimed that these two newspapers, and a number of others, had published false and defamatory matter about him, alleging several other serious offences, of which he had not been convicted. He was represented at the trial of the two libel actions by Serjeant Sullivan, an Irish barrister and the last holder of the obsolete senior rank of Serjeant to practise in England (but in full use in the days of Charles Dickens; see the trial of Bardell v. Pickwick in the Pickwick papers).

Hewart obviously, and predictably, at once formed a strongly adverse view of Hobbs, which his counsel was incapable of dislodging. Hewart's attitude communicated itself to the 'special' jury, with whom he was sitting. When the hearing of Hobbs' case against Tinling & Co.(the first of the two to be tried) was half-way through, the jury sent first a 'tentative intimation', and then a second message, to the judge, saying that they did not need to hear any more evidence, but wished to find for the defendants. Hewart showed neither of these messages to counsel, his first (elementary) mistake; he then, for no good reason, declined to allow Serjeant Sullivan to address the jury, and entered judgment for the defendants: two more mistakes. Next, he rejected Sullivan's application for an adjournment of the second action, made on the ground that Hobbs could not now have a fair second trial, in view of the adverse publicity about the first case: yet another mistake. At this Sullivan took umbradge, and left the Court, whereupon Hewart dismissed the second case as well; a fifth and last mistake.

Hobbs, no doubt on Sullivan's advice, appealed to the Court of Appeal,[14] a redoubtable trio consisting of Scrutton, Greer and Sankey LJJ. He sought, and obtained, orders for new trials, on the grounds that Hewart had not given him fair hearings, and had made a number of procedural mistakes. The Court of Appeal, in the course of three unusually long judgments (28, 10 and 7 pages respectively) made serious criticisms of Hewart's conduct of the hearing.

Scrutton L.J., a famously and scrupulously correct commercial judge, said:

'I regret to say I do not think (Hobbs) had ... a trial according to the rules of law.'

Greer L.J. said percipiently: 'The Lord Chief Justice was too greatly influenced by the unfavourable opinion he had formed of the plaintiff'.

Sankey L.J., a future Lord Chancellor, with whom Hewart was later to cross swords in the House of Lords said: 'The case required careful and patient investigation, which it did not receive.'

Considering that the Court of Appeal was dealing with, and upholding, an appeal based on the allegation that the Lord Chief Justice had not given fair trials to an aggrieved litigant, these are strong words indeed.

The portrait by Oswald Birley of 1935, when in post as Chief Justice, shows him at his desk in, probably typical,

14 Reported as Hobbs v. Tinling Co. Ltd [1929] 1 K.B. 1, which Stevens, op. cit. p33n, cryptically asserts is not a report 'in its full form'.

Lord Hewart C.J. By Oswald Birley, the embodiment of badness in judges.

cantankerous mood. This image seems to me to show, with presumably unintentional accuracy, the general perception of a Bad Judge; so I have asked my graphic artist friend, Victoria Wharton, to adapt it for use as the cover of this book. He is depicted, looking typically grumpy, sitting in his chambers surrounded by books and papers, and wearing, again typically, but quite inappropriately, a full-bottomed wig and ceremonial robes, no doubt to emphasize his eminence and importance.

He retired in 1940, was surprisingly and for no good reason, advanced to a Viscountcy in the same year, and died 3 years later, a thoroughly Bad Judge.

CHAPTER FIVE

Another Very Bad 20th Century Judge

I N THE YEARS SHORTLY BEFORE I EMBARKED on practice at the bar in 1960, there were several very bad High Court, and County Court, judges. Many of the latter had been Judges in the British Colonies, which were then gaining their independence and getting rid of their English Judges, who were regarded as part of the former Colonial regime; they were known to the Bar as 'Jungle Judges'.

Probably the worst Judge in the 1950s (though not a Jungle Judge) was Sir Hugh Imbert Periam Hallett. He was born in 1886; after education at Westminster and Christ Church, Oxford (he was President of the Union), he was called to the Bar by Inner Temple in 1911. He served in WWI and was awarded the Military Cross. He was the Recorder of Newcastle-upon-Tyne for only a year (which suggests a practice on the North-Eastern Circuit), before he was appointed to the High Court Bench (King's Bench Division) in 1939, at the age of 53, and in accordance with the practice, still current today, was knighted. So far, so creditable and reputable. But trouble lay ahead.

I have been kindly reminded by Sir Oliver Popplewell of the following anecdote, which I had not previously associated with Hallett J, but which exemplifies a few of his peculiar personal qualities. He was on circuit, out of London, with a marshal (a young barrister travelling, staying in the Judge's Lodgings, and sitting in Court, with the Judge, to gain experience). One evening the Judge was counting the small change in his pockets, and announced that it was 6 pence, then a small silver coin equivalent to 2 ½ 'new' pence, short. He thereupon began a minute search of the Lodgings for the missing coin, and required the marshal to assist him. After several fruitless hours of searching, over two evenings, the marshal got fed up, and rashly took a 6d piece from his own pocket, produced it to the Judge, and said with triumph that he had 'found it behind a cushion in the drawing room'. The Judge thanked him courteously; but alas, the following morning, he told the marshal very severely, that he had re-checked his accounts and found he had made a mistake in his calculations: he had not mislaid the 6d coin after all; the Marshall had lied to him about the coin he had said he had found, he could not continue as his marshal, and must at once return to London in ignominy. Might this have been a 'deliberate mistake and trap' to get rid of an uncongenial marshal? More serious bad judicial behaviour was to follow.

On the 21st of January 1953, a miner named Emlyn Jones was killed in an accidental roof-fall half a mile underground at Llay Main Colliery, Wrexham. A similar accident had occurred there not long before. His widow, Mary Myfanway, brought a civil claim for damages for negligence etc. against the National Coal Board: (we had a coal industry in those days). The counsel at the trial of her claim at Chester Assizes in July 1956 were two very experienced Welsh juniors: William Mars-Jones, a future QC and High Court Judge, appeared for Mrs Jones, and (recently deceased) Emlyn Hooson, a future M.P., QC (at 35) and Life Peer, for the Board. The judge was Hallett J. He dismissed Mrs Jones' claim on all points, just possibly rightly in law. But his conduct of the hearing was bad, particularly towards her counsel, and, when Mars-Jones was trying to cross-examine the Board's expert witness, it became even worse.

So bad that she took an appeal to the Court of Appeal, mainly on the basis that she had not had a fair trial, and that the judge had taken over her counsel's role in questioning the witnesses; a classic example of disregarding Lords Bacon and Greene's advice (supra).

A very high-powered panel of Lord Justices was assembled to hear the appeal, reported as *Jones v. National Coal Board* [1957] 2 Q.B.155: Denning (not yet a Lord, nor Master of the Rolls), Romer, and Parker (not yet a Lord, nor Chief Justice), LJJ., over 4 days in February and March 1957. Both sides had by now instructed leading counsel; Gerald Gardiner QC, a future Lord Chancellor and very formidable advocate, for Mrs Jones, and Edmund Davies QC, a future, and very popular, Lord Justice of Appeal, for the Board. The Court reserved its judgment for 24 days; then allowed Mrs Jones' appeal, because of Hallett J's misconduct, and ordered a new trial. The Court of Appeal was severely critical of Hallett's behaviour. Denning L.J. quoted Lord Bacon's famous remarks (see p.1 supra), and also a number of reported relevant cases, including *Yuill* (supra p.3), and the then most recent appellate decision, *R.v.Clewer* (1953) 37 C.A.R.37, of which case more below. It is the curious fact that all of the reports of the appeal hearing indicate that neither Gardiner nor Edmund Davies referred in argument to these or any other reported cases at all; perhaps they had the sang froid, borne of experience, to rely only on the transcripts of the trial, and their own advocacy.

The consequences of the success of Mrs Jones' appeal are described at page 174 of Prof. F.R.V.Heuston's book 'Lives of the Lord Chancellors 1940-1970' (Oxford 1987). The

Professor wrote (quoting from a book by Lord Denning) that Lord Chancellor Kilmuir, *né* Maxwell Fyfe, sent for the Judge. It was arranged that he should sit for a little while and then resign. This he did at the end of the summer term. All very, even perhaps too, gentlemanly. I hope Hallett did better during his last face-saving months. He was then in his early 70s.

But there are some surprising, and perhaps less than laudable, aspects of this story. The judge in the trial at Bedford Assizes in October 1952 of a Mr Clewer (referred to by Denning LJ: see above) for forgery was none other than Hallett J. Mr Clewer was convicted and sentenced to 3 years' imprisonment: he also appealed on the basis of Hallett's behaviour at his trial, which bore many similarities to that in Mrs. Jones' case. The Court of Criminal Appeal in *Clewer's* case was presided over by the then Lord Chief Justice, Lord Goddard. He and his colleagues (Byrne and Gerrard JJ.) were justifiably very severe in their criticism of Hallett's conduct, exemplified in the following extract from his remarks to prosecuting counsel, in the course of, and interrupting, defence counsel's closing speech to the jury:-

> 'When I come to sum up, I might or might not go into all these details which have made this case last into a third day; but I rather think I might not. I regard them very much as a dust [15] storm raised for the purpose of advocacy, mainly by defence counsel [Mr C.G.L.du Cann] but it is my duty as a judge to get the jury to see that they may do justice I think Mr du Cann thinks I am being offensive to him. I have really been admiring him. I have

15 It is tempting to engage in some amateur psychology, and to wonder whether Hallett's repeated (but inappropriate) references to 'dust storms', whatever they may be, derive from his sub-conscious recollection of Lord Greene's then recent warning in *Yuill* (supra p 3, 7 years earlier) against a Judge's 'vision [being] clouded by the dust of conflict'; but of course Hallett misused the metaphor about the wrong participant in the trial.

been watching advocates for years and years and have even been one myself. There are cases when raising a dust storm and seeing your client escape is the best advocacy. It requires skill and one sits admiring that skill being asserted; but I am not sure I am going to get entangled in any dust storm. I am more likely to tell the jury what are the facts they can infer, and if they think it right, that the forgery was done or brought about by this man.'

After reciting that bewildering and extraordinary passage of rambling and mixed metaphors, uttered by Hallett J. in the jury's presence, the Court of Criminal Appeal allowed Mr Clewer's appeal. But was it not Goddard's duty then to report Hallett's conduct, in a case involving the subject's liberty (of which he was, at least pending appeal, unjustly deprived), to the then Lord Chancellor, Simonds, as Denning LJ was to do three years later in Mrs Jones' civil case? If he had done so, might not the judge's injudicial behaviour have been ended sooner? I also wonder why Denning LJ, when referring to Clewer's case in the Court's judgment in Mrs Jones' case, did not mention that Hallett had 'form'. Is this perhaps a forgivable example of the criticism, often levelled at doctors, of 'closing ranks'? Denning probably foresaw that Hallett was for the chop; but even so, I think it ought not have been left to me to spot what he had said, or rather had not said, 56 years ago.

Hallett lived on in retirement, and died in 1967; he had been Treasurer of the Inner Temple in 1965. In my view he was, at least, by the early 1950s, a thoroughly Bad Judge.

CHAPTER SIX.

A Third Very Bad 20TH Century High Court Judge

I DID MY PUPILLAGE, IN 1959, in Chambers on the first floor of 12 King's Bench Walk in the Temple. It was, by the standards of the day, a good set with about a dozen members (minuscule by modern standards). The Head was one of the outstanding barristers then in practice, Gerald Gardiner QC. The chambers had the quaint habit (unthinkable now) of meeting for afternoon tea and biscuits at about 4pm in my pupil-master, Douglas Lowe's, fine room over-looking Inner Temple's garden, from an elegant bay window. [Lowe had been a track champion in 2 successive Olympic Games in the 1930s]. Gerald Gardiner seldom attended these gatherings; but when he did, there was greater formality in the air. I well remember him sipping his tea and complaining, in moderate but heart-felt language, that he had just been deprived of a very worth-while case, by the bad behaviour of the judge.

The case was *D. Badcock Ltd v. Middlesex County Council, the Central Electricity Generating Board and London County Council,* and the Judge was Roxburgh J, Sir Ronald Roxburgh, a judge since 1946 of the High Court, Chancery Division. It concerned a complaint by Badcocks (owners and operators of a fleet of large barges on the Thames in London) that the various Defendants had so polluted the water of the Thames, which was admitted to be a public Highway, as to corrode and so damage the bottoms of their barges. As can be easily imagined, this was a very sizable piece of litigation, with many issues of fact and law to be resolved. It needed exactly what it did not get – a patient and attentive judge: 'a well-tuned cymbal'. It also needed, and got, a formidable, and no doubt very expensive, cohort of lawyers and experts: barristers and solicitors. When the case eventually reached the Court of Appeal (as is recounted below) there were no fewer than seven QCs,[16] three junior counsel and several expensive solicitors, representing the three remaining parties: the plaintiffs had settled with C.E.G.B. at an early stage. Gerald Gardiner was the leading counsel for the London County Council.

But, alas, Roxburgh was neither patient nor attentive, and not well-tuned. He was, in Lord Bacon's words 'over-speaking'. Sir Robert Megarry, a retired Chancery Judge, practitioner, and a learned and very entertaining author, was not exaggerating when he described Roxburgh in general as 'free from taciturnity' (see above 'A New Miscellany-at-Law' p.114). Roxburgh repeatedly interrupted Badcock's QC's opening, and his examination of his witnesses. I remember being in Court as a mere observer, when the Judge, typically and peremptorily, demanded to be told whether or not the river Brent joined the Thames at Brentford, (which it did, and does), but which was wholly irrelevant to the point counsel was trying to deal with.

A further, and extreme, example occurred on the seventh day when Mr Badcock himself was giving his evidence-in-chief. The Judge repeatedly argued with Badcock's QC, as to whether his case could succeed, even if they proved everything they alleged. This argument was renewed and continued, in the middle of Mr Badcock's evidence-in-chief, up to and after the midday or luncheon break; a little later

16 They included one future Lord Chancellor, one future Lord Chief Justice, one future Lord Justice of Appeal, one former Attorney-General and one former Chairman of the Bar Council.

after the resumption, it was realised that Mr Badcock was still in the witness box, whereupon the Judge said (see [1960] 2 Ll.L.R at p63 left col.): 'You need not stay in the witness box. I meant to say that at lunchtime. You will probably never get back there.' Not a courteous, proper, impartial or encouraging remark at that stage, for Badcocks in particular; but entirely typical of Roxburgh.

After that, understandably but (as it turned out) ill-advisedly, Badcock and their lawyers despaired of getting the case properly and fairly heard. They came to the conclusion that the conduct and attitude of the judge was so hostile, and so prejudiced against, them, and the progress of the case was so slow, that they simply could not afford to continue to risk the huge legal costs of continuing the hearing: only the opening and three witnesses having been heard after eight days' hearing. They therefore 'submitted to judgment against them, with all the defendants' costs,'

This highly unusual step, even in the Chancery Division, (the direct result of Roxburgh's continuously injudicious conduct) gave rise to yet more complex litigation. Badcocks decided to appeal on the basis that they had not had, and had no prospect of having, a fair trial. Their Notice of Appeal (after amendment during the appeal hearing) included the following: they complained

> 'that the learned judge misdirected himself, decided wrongly in law, and wrongly exercised his discretion in the following respects:-
>
> 1(a) in holding that it was not open to the Plaintiffs on their Statement of Claim to base any part of their claim upon partial replacement of barge bottoms,
>   (b) when the Plaintiffs sought leave to amend their Statement of Claim by including an express claim for damages based on partial replacement of barge bottoms, in imposing terms, or

adversely intimating that he would not allow such amendments to be made except on terms, which were in the circumstances unreasonable and in law unjustifiable,

(c) in holding that the Statement of Claim as delivered was demurrable and disclosed no cause of action.

2. Because of the unreasonable attitude displayed by the learned judge throughout the hearing and the view found by him on erroneous grounds that the Plaintiffs' claim was misconceived, followed by the misdirections, wrong decisions and wrong exercises of discretion hereinbefore set out, there was no prospect by the end of the seventh day that the further hearing of the case would be fairly conducted by the learned judge, and in consequence further participation in the trial by the plaintiffs would serve no useful purpose, and the Plaintiffs were accordingly obliged to submit to judgment.'

In response to this Notice of Appeal, the L.C.C., with the support of Middlesex County Council, applied to the Court of Appeal to strike it out or set it aside, on the basis that, Badcocks, having submitted to judgment against themselves, could not possibly succeed in any appeal from that judgment. The hearing of this application in mid-July 1960, which failed, is reported in detail at [1960] 1 Ll.L.R. p. 245: the exchanges between the judges and counsel set out in full at pages 250 to 252 show all too vividly the legal tangle that Roxburgh's conduct had created.

During the later, substantive, hearing of the appeal, reported at [1960] Vol. 2 Ll.L.R.57, Badcocks were allowed to amend their Notice of Appeal as above. Their 'cri de coeur' was, alas, still confronted by the problem that they had unconditionally 'submitted to judgment' against themselves, and were therefore, in the language of insurance companies, 'the authors of their own misfortunes'. There was much learned argument deployed on the difference (if any) between 'submitting to judgment' and 'consenting to judgment' which latter was unquestionably final.

At least Evershed M.R. said in giving his judgment (at p.63 seq.),

> 'The experience of listening to the Judge's long and exacting criticism of the Statement of Claim was no doubt trying for Badcocks and their advisers. [Their leading counsel] made it quite clear that he was not suggesting any kind of deliberate unfairness or bias on the Judge's part. The high intelligence of the Judge is too well-known to make any such suggestion possible. It must, however, be accepted, as all the learned counsel experienced in cases before him told us, it was the Judge's practice[17] to take himself a large part of the conduct of his cases, though (as we were also informed) his interventions were not confined to the conduct of only one only of the parties to them. We are of the opinion that the learned judge's interventions went beyond what was either necessary or desirable'.

But in the end the Court of Appeal were unmoved: they dismissed the appeal with costs, and refused leave to appeal further to the House of Lords. Badcocks must have felt mightily aggrieved at their experience of litigation, and Gardiner did not enjoy his cup of tea.

Roxburgh had been appointed to the Bench in 1946 at the age of 57 by Lord Chancellor Jowett. At that time the quality of the judiciary of the Chancery Division was relitively low, with the consequence that the amount of litigation that reached trial was remarkably small, as is borne out by the relatively slim volumes of annual Law Reports that were published in those years. Litigants were under-

---

17 A very peculiar and undesirable one, in my respectful opinion, which would certainly not be approved by the modern Judicial Studies Board, and enough of itself to justify the judge's being reproved. It infringes virtually every one of Lord Bacon's recommendations.

standably chary of risking an expensive disaster, such as befell Badcocks. Roxburgh had had a large practice before the previous, much more 'user-friendly', generation of Chancery Judges. His background was education at Harrow and Trinity, Cambridge with a 1st class degree in Classics, followed by call to the Bar by Middle Temple. Rather oddly he became a Bencher of another Inn, Lincoln's Inn in 1957, and was its Treasurer in 1957. He retired from the Chancery Bench in 1960 and died in 1981.

He was a very Bad Judge, a view confirmed to me by a now retired Chancery practitioner and Court of Appeal Judge, who had much personal experience of Roxburgh; he told me that Roxburgh had the knack, peculiar to really Bad Judges, of sending all the parties to a piece of litigation, including the winners, away dissatisfied.

CHAPTER SEVEN

A Very Bad 20TH Century Circuit Judge

S UPPOSE IT IS FEBRUARY 1968, and then suppose you are a quite young and inexperienced barrister, called Gardner (not Gardiner), appearing for the last of a group of three London criminals: Hircock, Farmer and Leggett. The case against your client, on joint charges with the other two, of theft from, and assault on, a petrol station attendant, is not strong. Your client's case is that he took no part in the assault, but remained in Hircock's car, 'otherwise engaged' with his girlfriend. After all the evidence has been called, and counsel for the prosecution, and for the first two accused men, have made their final speeches to the jury, you rise nervously to your feet to make your final speech — the fourth the Judge and the jury will have heard that day.

The Crown's case against your client is different from, and weaker than, that against the others; but even so, there is not much for you to say that has not been said at least once before. But it is your duty to your client to do your best for him. So you start your speech.

The Judge thereupon places his robed forearms on top of each other on the bench in front of him, and then his bewigged head on his forearms, and emits a loud groan, followed very audibly by the words: 'Oh God!' addressed to nobody in particular, if not the Deity. You decide, rightly but with some courage, to try to continue your speech, even at the risk of eliciting more judicial discourtesy and mild blasphemy. Sure enough, the judge continues more than once to sigh, groan, and invoke divine intervention.

The jury, who have themselves taken oaths to attend to the evidence and give verdicts accordingly, do not know whether to laugh sycophantically, or pretend not to have noticed the judge's shocking behaviour. They are certainly not being encouraged to pay much attention to what you have said to them. After you have finished, the Judge delivers a cursory and world-weary summing up. After a short retirement the jury return to Court, and deliver verdicts of Guilty against all three accused persons on both charges; the judge sentences them all to 30 months' imprisonment.

If you had been more senior or more experienced, what you might have done, what counsel who knew of this Judge's habitual bad behaviour did; is, at the first groan, to enquire solicitously after the judge's health, call the court usher to fetch a glass of water for the judge to drink, sit down and decline to continue, until he invites you to do so, and maybe realises that two can play at his game; in that way you can make sure his behaviour is all noted in the court record. But you are probably not senior enough to dare to do anything like that, in case you find yourself in professional trouble for disrespectful behaviour.

Few London criminal practitioners, now aged about 60 or more, will need to be told that the above learned Judge was, to give him his full entitlement of titles, His Honour Judge the Honourable Ewen Edwin Samuel Montagu, Queen's Counsel, (O.B.E., later unmeritoriously advanced to C.B.E.), the Senior Judge sitting in the spacious Court in Parliament Square, then used by Middlesex Area Quarter Sessions. [Now transformed for, and used by, the new Supreme Court, the successor of the House of Lords in its Judicial capacity].

Montagu was the second of the three sons of a very wealthy banker, who, on acquiring a peerage, had discarded the surname Swaythling, in favour of the name Montagu (one of his brothers, an active Communist, had distinction in promoting the game of Ping-Pong). He was educated at Westminster, and at Harvard and Cambridge Universities, where he had his own valet. He was called to the Bar by Middle Temple in 1924, and took silk in 1939.

During and after WWII he became quite famous (he fancied, even world-famous), and was deservedly decorated, for his conspicuous part in the so-called Operation Mincemeat. This was the elaborate scheme, propounded in 1943 to deceive, as it did, the German High Command into thinking that the Allies were planning to invade mainland Greece and Sardinia, and not, as was their actual, and eventually successful plan, to invade Sicily, and thence Italy. This interesting episode was described in a book, and then a film, called 'The Man who Never Was', both of which were very popular. Fortunately for Operation Mincemeat, Montagu's part in it did not require either patience or courtesy.

After the War he returned to the Bar and in the 1960s was appointed as a Judge of a then anomalous rank: not of the High Court, nor of the County Court, but (with perhaps as many as a dozen others) of one of the London Criminal Courts, of rather lower status than the permanent Old Bailey Judges. For some unknown reason they expected to be, and were, addressed as 'My Lord', an appellation strictly appropriate only for High Court, and even higher, Judges.

The three convicted men appeal to the Court of Appeal, presided over by Lord Chief Justice Widgery, saying that they did not have a fair trial. Widgery said that 'your client Leggett's case required rather special care and consideration' (which it certainly did not get from the Judge). Widgery and his colleagues nevertheless contrived to uphold all the convictions, by drawing a specious distinction between 'discourtesy and impatience', which they deplored, but were prepared to excuse, and 'conduct which positively and actively obstructs counsel in the doing of his work'. They contrived to distinguish your case from Clewer's case (supra p 43) because, they said, in that case, but not in yours, 'there was an invitation to the jury to disregard what was being said, and active, positive interference with counsel in the pursuit of his task'. However, despite finding it difficult to say that 'the sentences were wrong as passed' (whatever those words may mean), they felt 'sufficient doubt about them to make it desirable to reduce them in some measure' The sentences on your client and the second accused man were reduced from 30 to 18 months, which may well have meant they were released at once: in modern slang 'a cop-out'.

I regard that whole episode, in both Courts, (reported as *R. v Hircock, Farmer and Leggett* [1970] 1 QB 67) as callow and deplorable; in particular that Montagu's disgraceful behaviour received only mild disapprobation, secondly, because of the bogus supposed distinction from Clewer's case, (Montagu's behaviour was bound, to use Widgery's words, 'actively to obstruct counsel in his work' by distracting him from carrying out his work) and lastly the unexplained, and on the Court's view, quite unjustified, reduction in two of the sentences, assuming as the Appeal Court had decided, that the men were rightly convicted: all amounting to the failure to address a serious issue of judicial malpractice, by intellectual feebleness. It is also the deplorable fact that this case was not the first in which Montagu's behaviour was strongly criticised by the Court of Appeal. Ewen Montagu was a distinguished, active and conspicuous member of the London Jewish community.

I have been told by Mr Ivan Lawrence QC, himself a distinguished member of the Jewish community, that Montagu's conduct in Court was consistently worse, when Jewish counsel were appearing before him, than when he had Gentiles as counsel in his Court. As a mere Gentile, I can only report that I found appearing in his Court a deeply unpleasant experience. Mr Lawrence had appeared before Montagu in 1966, and had been treated with the Judge's usual discourtesy. His client was convicted of living on immoral earnings and was sentenced to imprisonment. Mr Lawrence advised him to appeal, as he did, and also to be represented by leading counsel: Mr Malcolm Morris QC. The Appeal Court refused to allow the appeal on the grounds of Montagu's bad behaviour, which it rather feebly deplored, but held he had misdirected the jury on an issue relating to the burden of proof. So the appeal was allowed. Montagu had a charmed life.[18]

Experience showed that the only way of dealing with Ewan Montagu was to give him the same discourtesy that he routinely gave to the Bar. Like many bullies, he could not take the sort of treatment he gave to others. The best exponent of this was Harold Cassel, a tall and imposing barrister, who was himself wealthy enough not to be bothered with pleasing or displeasing solicitors (and consequently won their respect). He often appeared in Montagu's court, and would address the jury, standing with one foot raised on the seat beside him, and while gazing in a lordly fashion at the ceiling of the Court. This, as he well knew, irritated the Judge beyond measure. 'Mr. Cassel,' Montagu would say testily, 'will you pay the jury the compliment of looking at them, when you

18   R. v. Ptohopoulos (1967) Vol. 52 C.A.R.47

are speaking to them?' 'Certainly, my Lord,' Cassel would reply, with a gracious smile, 'is there any particular member of the jury your Lordship would like me to look at?' Montagu had no answer to that. Ironically, when Cassel himself went on the Bench, he was, I am told, another very difficult Judge.

Montagu would also, I believe, after a more than usually quarrelsome day in Court, seek to ingratiate himself with counsel in their robing-room, perhaps realising that even he had gone too far. But of course no-one wanted to talk to him, and the robing-room would empty rapidly.

I confess to being unimpressed by the uninformed compliments about him as judge, which almost always appear as the last chapter of the various books, about his exploits in Operation Mincemeat.

He eventually retired in 1969, to the relief of the London Criminal Bar, and died in 1985.

CHAPTER EIGHT

Two More Bad Circuit Judges.

THE CIRCUIT JUDGE WAS THE INVENTION OF Dr, later Lord, Beeching and his colleagues, in their radical Report of their Royal Commission into the age-old system of Criminal Justice, especially outside London. They reported in 1969, to the effect that the long-established Courts of Assizes and Quarter Sessions should be abolished.[19] These Courts were indeed abolished and replaced on 1st January 1972 by a new kind of Court, called the Crown Court, in which a new kind of Judge now sits, called a Circuit Judge (a misleading title, since they did not, and do not, go 'on circuit'). They deal with the great bulk of the more serious criminal cases in England & Wales. There are at the time of writing over 600 Circuit Judges (so many that Whitaker's Almanac has given up listing them all by name); so it is not surprising that a few have proved to be thoroughly Bad, despite the modern system of selection, training and 'probationary' sitting, prior to permanent appointment.

HIS HONOUR JUDGE GWYN R.F. MORRIS QC

Who's Who and Who was Who are fascinating and valuable books of reference for the amateur researcher. Both are substantially written by the persons included, about

---

19 this episode is dealt with in detail in my previous book, Death of a Circuit, of 2006

themselves, who are invited every year to provide up-to-date information. Who was Who consists of the deceased's last entry pre-mortem, reprinted. What is included is obviously of primary interest, often on more than one level; but what is excluded is often almost as significant as what is put in. Thus an individual who informs Posterity that he read Law (aka Jurisprudence) at Oxford, and got a First class degree, not only is obviously very bright, but also wants Posterity to know it. Gwyn Morris saw fit to omit from his entry, not only his mother's and first wife's names, but also any details of his education prior to his membership of New College, Oxford. Perhaps he was ashamed of both his mother his first wife and his school. He was certainly not ashamed of his second wife's family: we learn that she was Lady Audrey Ingestre, the sister of the 21st Earl of Shrewsbury.

Gwyn Morris QC, was the Head of the set of Chambers, on the first floor of Goldsmith Building (over-looking the Temple Churchyard), whence I started practice in January 1960. It was, by the standards of the day, a middle-sized and middle-ranking set, with one silk (Morris had taken silk in 1958) and six or seven juniors, including one or two part-timers. Morris ran the set in a wholly autocratic way: we had no chambers meetings to discuss matters of general concern, such as possible new members, chambers finances, etc. You got to know that a new barrister had joined the set, only if and when you happend to see the sign-writer painting his name at the entrance to the chambers. The barristers and staff were all men; the only female was the typist/telephonist. As a callow 25 year-old, I assumed this was entirely normal, as indeed it was; my pupillage chambers (see chapter 5 above) had seemed to be much the same. But a wind of change was beginning to blow through the Temple. The 'rules' governing the number of silks there could be in any one set were relaxed in the mid-'60s, and more women were coming to the Bar. Democracy arrived and changed the Bar for good – in every sense.

This was not to Gwyn Morris' liking; we had one disagreeable chambers meeting, shortly after which the chambers underwent a very painful, public and expensive split. I was one of the emigrants; we were lucky to find excellent rooms at 13 King's Bench Walk, where I spent the rest of my time at the Bar, including 10+ years as the third Head of Chambers. In that burdensome capacity, whenever I had a decision to take, I used to consider what Gwyn Morris would have done, and then I did the opposite. We had no serious problems in those latter years, but we eventually found very handsome new posher rooms in Beaumont Street for our Oxford premises, much smarter than our previous cramped space there over a ladies' hair-dressers.

Shortly after his Chambers split in half, Gwyn Morris, despite bad health, took a job as a permanent Judge at the Old Bailey, where he was predictably unpopular. There was an entertaining incident when he, and the Head of the new emigrant set were both sitting at the Old Bailey, the latter as Recorder. They had cordially disliked each other for many years, and both noticed that they had been given places next to each other at the Court Luncheon Table, a formal occasion. Both of them gave instructions, to different officials, that their places should be changed, with the consequence that they were both moved, and found themselves sitting side-by-side at the other end of the table.

It was only a question of time before Morris' conduct of a run-of-the-mill trial, and his temperament, however successful for an advocate, showed themselves as quite inappropriate for the every-day conduct of a criminal trial. In 1972 two naive Scotsmen, visiting London on business, unwisely decided to have their dinner in a basement restaurant in Frith Street, Soho. They found themselves entertaining two 'so-called hostesses', who ordered plentiful and expensive food and drink. At the end of their visit they were given a bill for the then exorbitant amount of £68. This they refused to pay: and they were then assaulted by the doorman and a waiter, and relieved of £50, which was all the money they had with them.

They went to the police, with the consequence that the doorman and the waiter were charged, and sent for trial for robbery and assault at the Old Bailey. Their trial, before Judge Gwyn Morris QC and a jury, ended on February 2nd 1973, with their being convicted by a majority of ten to two, of robbery and sentenced to three year's imprisonment. [The report of their appeal at *R. V. Hulusi and another*, Vol. 58 CAR 378 does not indicate what happened to the assault allegation.]

They appealed to the Criminal Division of the Court of Appeal, presided over by Lawton L.J., a very experienced and respected judge of criminal cases, sitting with two also experienced High Court Judges, Nield and Eveleigh JJ. Lawton's judgment effectively consists of a continuous catalogue of severe criticisms of Morris' conduct of the case at every stage. Lawton L.J. described it as 'a simple case (where) in the ordinary way the prospects of a successful defence would have been poor.' But Morris had repeatedly interrupted the evidence, in the jury's presence, he unfairly rebuked counsel who was representing both accused men, and 'took over' the questioning of witnesses before counsel on either side had had a chance to conduct the case themselves. At one stage he remarked sarcastically to counsel that he doubted whether they were involved in the same case. The Appeal Court accepted the appellants' submission that 'the judge's constant criticisms [of the appellants' counsel] may very well have led the jury to think that [he] was in some way behaving in a tricky manner, the object of which was to mislead them.' It is difficult to find any part of the judgment which does not contain a serious adverse opinion of this judge's conduct of, and in, the trial.

Prosecuting counsel obviously agreed with the Court of Appeal's view. The report laconically records that (with the Court's concurrence) he 'did not seek to support the conviction': in consequence the accused men were released, probably luckily.

This very severe rebuke may have had a salutary effect upon Judge Morris. At least the Reports do not carry any further instances of judicial misbehaviour by him. He continued to sit at the Old Bailey, retired in 1981, and died in 1982.

HER HONOUR JUDGE DEBORAH ROWLAND

Much adverse publicity is frequently given in the media to the huge imbalance of the sexes in the higher judiciary. It is undoubtedly true that even now there are far fewer women on the Circuit Bench, and the higher reaches of the Judicial Hierarchy, than would reflect their numbers in the population. This silly contention ignores the obvious fact that the pool of barristers and solicitors from which appointments are made included, until very recently, far more men than women. The imbalance is now being rapidly corrected, but it will still require the passage of a number of years before the necessary experience is accumulated by the recently recruited women. However I suspect that the (recently abolished) Lord Chancellor's Department attempted in the mid-'70s to correct the imbalance too fast and made a number of appointments of women to the 'new' Circuit Bench, before the present, more rigorous, process of selection was introduced. Most of these were at least satisfactory. A very few were conspicuously unsuccessful. One of these was Deborah Rowland, the (possibly fictitious) account of whose appointment deserves inclusion here: it has, to my mind, the ring of truth.

She was born in 1913. She had none of the conventional education for a lawyer, or a judge. Her entry in Who was Who records only her attendance at the Slade School of Art and the Courtauld Institute of Fine Art, where she obtained a diploma in Fine Art and Architecture. But in her 30s she made a sharp and surprising career change. She was called to the Bar by Lincoln's Inn in 1950, at the relatively advanced age for that era of 37, practiced for some 15 or so years, and then in her 50s, applied for appointment to the Circuit Bench, at or about the time of its creation.

In those days there was a probationary post of Deputy Circuit Judge for those who aspired to the Bench as Circuit Judge, or as Recorder. Deborah Rowland, who was a competent practitioner, but with little, if any experience of the extraordinary complexities of Landlord and Tenant, or Housing, litigation, applied successfully for appointment as a Circuit Judge, reasonably expecting to sit to hear, as a Deputy, cases within her areas of experience. I can personally vouch, from my own experience, for the rather over-optimistic, even haphazard, way in which Deputy Circuit Judges (of whom I was, for a time, one) were at that time called upon to try, civil and criminal cases, of all shapes and sizes, irrespective of their personal experience or expertise. I recall being called upon to hear a complex Bankruptcy case at Chesterfield Court (a topic of which I knew virtually nothing), and to sentence at Reading two persons for armed robbery (an offence now usually dealt with by a High Court or senior Circuit Judge).

But unhappily, she was confronted one day with a Landlord & Tenant case, which raised an obscure, but important, legal issue, which it fell to her to decide. Luckily, one of the parties was represented by a barrister who was an acknowledged expert in the relevant area. He prepared an elaborate written Skeleton Argument advancing his client's case, in a series of numbered paragraphs. This is now commonplace, indeed in many cases compulsory; but it was then uncommon, but often helpful to the judge trying the case.

Deputy Circuit Judge Rowlands found it very helpful, so helpful that in her judgment she adopted, but without express acknowledgment, the contentions and arguments set out in the numbered paragraphs of the Skeleton, and found in favour of its author's client. The losing party appealed, but was unsuccessful. One of the appellate judges ended his judgment with words of commendation to the following effect:

'We would not wish to part with this case without paying tribute to the learned and felicitous way in which the learned Deputy Judge dealt with the complexities of this case, by summarising the obscure legal position in logical steps, and coming to an unimpeachable conclusion.' This was, of course, counsel's Skeleton Argument, revamped. She was very shortly afterwards, in 1971, granted a full-time appointment in the County Court, in the next year to be transformed into the Circuit Bench.

She had not the professional detachment necessary for

the proper discharge of the judicial function; she was known to shed tears of distress in Court when she had, as judges dealing with family disputes frequently have, to deal with bitter family litigation, frequently involving children. She was, I fear, a bad judge. She died in office in 1986, having served her 15 years on the Bench, but did not live to enjoy her retirement.

Rather sadly, but I think significantly, her recreations are listed in Who was Who, as 'Music' (she was a founder of the Bar Musical Society) 'painting and sculpture'. One cannot avoid the conclusion that her true metier was in the Arts, but not on the Bench; and that she would have made a good artist, rather than a poor (even bad) Judge.

Epilogue

So there they are: nine men and one woman, all of whom must, in their various ways and in my opinion, be regarded to a greater or lesser degree as Bad Judges. I warned you, even before you began to read it, that this would be a short book. There have of course been many other poor, or even bad, Judges. What is perhaps surprising is that, despite the repeated protests and exhortations of the Criminal Division of the Court of Appeal, the same elementary mistakes of impatience and arrogance continue to be made. Even in such elevated jurisdictions as The Old Bailey, there have been some pretty Bad Judges, only one of whom I have included.

I was heartened to read, reprinted in the Inner Temple's Yearbook for 2012 at pages 18-19 in the valedictory address of Sir Anthony (until recently Lord Justice) Hooper, that in his long experience at the criminal Bar, as a High Court Judge, and a Lord Justice of Appeal often sitting in the Court of Appeal, Criminal Division, was that the standard of judicial conduct had significantly improved since the 1970s. I think it is worth recording here that, when proper Criminal Appeals were first introduced (in 1907, when as a result of a notorious miscarriage of justice, the Court of Criminal Appeal was created) they were usually heard by Courts consisting of three High Court Judges, often, but by no means always including the Lord Chief Justice. So in some of the less serious cases (irrespective of their legal difficulty) the Judges were often adjudicating upon decisions and sentences made by their colleagues, whom they were understandably reluctant to differ and even more reluctant to criticise. For this reason in the 1960s the CCA was abolished, and the Criminal Division of the Court of Appeal created in its place. Sittings of that Court are now always presided over by the Lord Chief Justice or a Lord Justice of Appeal (such as Sir Anthony); and hence the status of that court has been much enhanced, and the appellate reluctance to criticise trial judges has been properly reduced.

It is however possible to detect a slight, but important, change in the Appeal Court's attitude to the conduct, and misconduct, of trial judges, particularly in Criminal cases, and in their behaviour towards advocates, who may now-a-days of course be solicitors (some with plenty of advocacy experience) or barristers (whose particular expertise ought to be advocacy). This welcome change can be discerned in the sparsely reported cases of *R. v. Lashley* and *R.v. Dickens*[2006] Crim. Law Review 783 and 881. These were two appeals both heard on 28th July 2005 from convictions before the same (unidentified) Circuit Judge by the same strong Court of Appeal, presided over by Judge LJ, the future Lord Chief Justice. They allowed both appeals (and refused retrials) in those cases where an unidentified Circuit Judge had treated counsel, throughout the trials, with a combination of discourtesy and patronising dispraise. The judgment of the Appeal Court in Lashley contains this important passage:

'Times have changed from when it was held that "discourtesy, even gross discourtesy by the Court to counsel, however regrettable, is not ground for quashing a conviction"'.

In other, less periphrastic, language, the Court was indicating a less tolerant approach towards judicial rudeness, such as Judge Ewan Montagu QC had been allowed to get away with. Evan so, there continue to be depths of badness which it is shocking to read about, and hard to reconcile with a proper judicial disposition. As recently as April 2008 an unidentified Circuit Judge took such exception to the inexperienced questioning of a witness by a young (female) barrister on an issue of identity that during the overnight adjournment of a trial he went to the trouble of preparing a document to be given to the barrister, in the jury's absence but the accused's presence, before the case resumed. It was headed 'the six Ps' and read as follows 'Prior Planning Prevents Piss Poor Performance'. I find it difficult to imagine the mentality of a Judge, who can so lamentably, and rudely, show his contempt for Counsel and desire to humiliate her in front of her client. This document was preceded by and the culmination of a campaign of interruption, which the Court of Appeal regarded as bound to convey the impression to the Accused man that he is not receiving a fair trial: the conviction was quashed.

Despite such incidents, I think we can be justifiably proud that, among the various failings of our English and Welsh judges, perhaps the worst failing of all does not appear, and has not appeared for very many years, namely Corruption. Some of our Judges may be, or may have been, impatient, discourteous, irritable, pompous, lazy, self-satisfied or simply wrong; but in my, and my contemporaries', experience of the second half of the 20th century, I do not think there has ever been any suggestion that a decision was arrived at by a corrupt motive, whether in relation to personal advantage or preferment, or in respect of some political or other cause. I speak here of judges of every rank, from the humblest

Tribunal to the lofty Supreme Court.

When we consider the public attitude to the Judiciary in very many other jurisdictions, some not very far away geographically, this has to be a remarkable achievement. It was by no means always thus. We do not need to believe in any special virtue attaching to Judges in England & Wales, or those in Scotland or Northern Ireland to account for their estimable probity. The probable explanation is, I fear, far more mundane, namely Money. In what is quaintly called the 'Early Modern Period', that is, the 16TH, 17TH and 18TH centuries, the judges received very substantial sums from the perquisites of their offices in 'fees and the sale of offices' as it is politely put by Robert Stevens (op. cit.p.50). Indeed much of that excellent book is devoted to the various tussles between the Judges (High Court, County Court and Scottish) on the one hand, and the Treasury on the other, in the 'Modern Modern Period', that is, over the period between the early 19th and the late 20th[t] centuries, which of course included the radical reforms of the Courts in the 1870s.

In 1832 the High Court Judges were paid £5,000 p.a., having been reduced by £500 in that year. I believe this figure (paltry by today's values) was then regarded as large enough to withstand the temptations of corrupt increase. The remarkable fact is that rate of remuneration had remained substantially unchanged until late in the 20th century. In the current (2012) edition of Whitaker's Almanack the annual salary of each High Court Judge, of whom there are now about 100, is listed as £172,753; the 36 Lord Justices of Appeal (the Appeal Court Judges) receive £196,707. Even higher salaries are paid to the Heads of the 3 Divisions, Chancery, Queen's Bench, and Family, and to the Lord Chief Justice. I am no arithmetician, but a computer seems to tell me that the 1832 figure has been increased by a remarkable factor of nearly 35, in the space of less than 200 years. Moreover there are about 100 High Court Judges at present, whereas less than 50 years ago, there were only about 50. So compared with other areas of public expense, the amounts in question are not large. But the quality of the judiciary, and the degree of public confidence in it, must be amongst the most crucial features of a modern democracy

There is only one area in which it could, and I think must, be recorded that public disquiet has called for, and received, a measure of reassurance against the possible risk of a want of impartiality in the Judiciary (I choose my words as carefully as possible); and that area is Freemasonry. It is common knowledge, and I think would not be disputed, that very many in the police service, and in both the solicitors' branch of the legal profession, and at the Bar, and amongst barristers' and judges' clerks, are active Freemasons. There are, I believe, many Freemasons at the Old Bailey, as in many other institutions of the City of London. I know of only one historic occasion when an overt attempt was made by a litigant to invoke his membership of a Masonic lodge to influence a judge's decision, the Judge being known to be also a mason, when the notorious Dr Crippen was about to be sentenced (to death) for the murder of his wife; this was obviously an extreme case and the attempt failed. Crippen was hanged.

However much more recently, I think some time in the '80s of the last century, the Lord Chancellor's Department introduced a question, which every applicant for any judicial post was required to answer: namely 'are you a Freemason?' It was explicit that a failure to answer this question would of itself disqualify the applicant from success in the application, and that the answer Yes or No would not help or hinder the application's [20]success.

I know of more than one Freemason judge, against whom of course no suggestion of impropriety was ever made. It would be interesting to know whether any similar provision is made in other Jurisdictions, European or Commonwealth, or in the United States.

There is of course no ground for complacency. In our area of enquiry, as in so many others, the price of good justice is eternal vigilance. Bad Judges, however few there may be, will always be a stain on the public perception of Justice.

20 I answered 'No'

List of Illustrations

Bibliography

Atlay, J.B.; *The Victorian Chancellors*. London. (1908)

Bacon, Lord Francis; *The Essayes or Counsels; Of Judicature*. (1625)

Bosanquet, Sir Ronald QC; *The Oxford Circuit*, London. (1951)

Heuston, Prof. F.R.V.; *Lives of the Lord Chancellors*. Oxford. (1987)

Harvey, C.P.; *The Advocate's Devil*. (1958)

Megarry, Sir Robert; *A New Miscellany-at-Law*. (2005)

Pannick, (Lord) David; *Judges*. (1987)

Stevens, Robert; *The Independence of the Judiciary*. (1993)

Various Authors; *ODNB, Who's Who, Who was Who*.

Williams, Graeme; *Death of a Circuit*. London.(2006)

General Index